Aesop's Human Zoo

Phædrus

Aesop's Human Zoo

ROMAN STORIES ABOUT OUR BODIES

Translated from Phaedrus's Latin by
JOHN HENDERSON

With Illustrations by Thomas Bewick

University of Chicago Press
Chicago and London

JOHN HENDERSON is professor of classics at the University of Cambridge and fellow of Kings College. He has published many books, including *Fighting for Rome* and *Telling Tales on Caesar.*

The University of Chicago Press, Chicago 60637
The University of Chicago Press, Ltd., London

Printed in the United States of America

13 12 11 10 09 08 07 06 05 04   5 4 3 2 1

ISBN (cloth): 0-226-32681-0

Library of Congress Cataloging-in-Publication Data

Phaedrus.
Aesop's human zoo : Roman stories about our bodies / translated from Phaedrus's Latin by John Henderson ; with illustrations by Thomas Bewick.
p. cm.
ISBN 0-226-32681-0 (cloth : alk. paper)
1. Phaedrus—Translations into English. 2. Fables, Latin—Translations into English. 3. Body, Human—Poetry. 4. Animals—Poetry. 5. Rome—Poetry. 6. Fables, Latin. I. Henderson, John, 1948– II. Bewick, Thomas, 1753–1828. III. Title.
PA6564.E5H455 2004
2003070288

∞ The paper used in this publication meets the minimum requirements of the American National Standard for Information Sciences—Permanence of Paper for Printed Library Materials, ANSI Z39.48-1992.

Contents

Preface

I

Aesop was the founder. His genre
I have polished in casual verse.

My book's double game: laugh-raiser
plus morals—canny folks' life-saver.

Is a hate campaign to anyone's taste—
"He has t r e e s talk, besides beasts of the zoo"?

Remember: I'm fun. And fables are fiction.

: : :

Aesopus auctor quam materiam repperit,
hanc ego poliui uersibus senariis.

Duplex libelli dos est: quod risum mouet
et quod prudentis uitam consilio monet.

Calumniari siquis autem uoluerit,
quod arbores loquantur, non tantum feræ,

fictis iocari nos meminerit fabulis.

Let's begin at the beginning, with this Preface.

As you see, Phaedrus starts with Aesop. His own job is to *polish* the fables, in conversational verse. He promises counsel rolled into humor.

As he does so, he tells us that he speaks, already, with forked tongue. He is playing a "double-edged" game, of "duplicity" (*duplex*). Tricksy Greek had a two-in-one word for it—*spoudaio-geloion,* which means "fusing seriousness with play."

It is perfectly true that, when fabulists talk the talk, their speciality is indeed the business of making "things" talk. Trees *will* indeed talk (see **37**). But this prefatory scrap is Phaedrus establishing his "Aesopic" credentials. A whispering wood can make a fearful image of the power of rumor, to do damage irrepressibly, unseizably, beyond reprisal. And, at once, Phaedrus is put upon, victimized, misunderstood, defiant—and (instructively) silly. This is part and parcel of setting up to tell fables. It can make you a target for all comers: they target you, for (allegedly) targeting victims, camouflaged by the forest cover. So the disclaimer marks out the territory for malice, in a first strike for retaliation. Welcome to heroic mockery—and mock heroics?

As you see, the fabulous Greek legend of the downtrodden slave Aesop was "back then." So far as we Romans are concerned, the fable-writing ex-slave writer Phaedrus is "now."

Will Fable adapt to the changes? Or survive? Write on, Phaedrus, and we'll find out what happens to Fable when it's written, in Latin.

First things first, though. We need an introduction.

Introduction

Phaedrus's Fables

Here are stories right from the very heart of Roman civilization. From the palace of Augustus, first emperor of Rome, no less. Most of them are completely unknown today. They bring us alongside Romans in an unusually genial and relaxed mood. These are short stories for fun. Their readers are allowing themselves to be tickled. Entertainment like this doesn't grow on trees in Classical Literature.

The author tells us his name, Phaedrus. And the manuscript that preserves most of his stories, together with remarks he volunteers himself, tells us he was a onetime slave of Augustus who turned *Aesop's Fables* into five books of Latin verse in the reign of Augustus's successor, Tiberius, between 30 and 40 A.D. We know of him only what little he decides to tell us. He is the ringmaster of the *Fables*, no more, no less.

Besides the animal fables we must be expecting, Greek collections of *Aesop's Fables* included a fair number of stories and anecdotes with everyday-life situations and occasional odds and ends of popular lore. Phaedrus expanded the range still wider, with satirical squibs and even stories set at Rome (see Further Reading, p. 121). But his fables have had a bumpy ride into our modern world. I must tell the tale of his tales, right away.

Phaedrus comes down to us, essentially, through the survival of a single ninth-century "Carolingian" manuscript ("P," see Further Reading. Its sibling was lost in a disastrous eighteenth-century fire at Rheims Abbey). This was written out as if in prose; and it was seriously mutilated, with fables in fragmentary ruins (see note on **8–9**) and huge chunks of at least books 2 and 5 missing (see note on **42**). Fortunately for us, Niccolò Perotti, a fifteenth-century Italian bishop, gathered many fables (from books 2 through 5) into an anthology, and these included, besides plenty we already have from Phaedrus, thirty more that are otherwise lost. They have been rather tinkered with, and shuffled, but they were at least passed on as verse. When these stories are weeded from the collection, we nickname them "Perotti's Appendix" (see Further Reading). There are plenty of really catchy tales that we only know from the "Appendix," and a fair number of them feature in the present selection.

But Phaedrus is in fact a sleeping giant who lurks behind the *Aesops* we all grew up with. In the medieval period, a set of selections from his *Fables* were redone in prose. Variously rewritten, reordered, and infiltrated with fables from other sources, these were widely disseminated through Europe, leaving us many manuscripts from the tenth century onward. Eventually, they fed printed editions, not least William Caxton's, and in this form founded the modern repertoire of Fable. When Phaedrus was rediscovered as the sixteenth century closed, giants such as La Fontaine, L'Estrange, and Lessing could choose how to mix the staple medieval selection with Phaedrus's own verses. A selection of fables derived from Phaedrus in this way also star in this book (see Further Reading).

Besides losing his status of "poet" in this staggered process of world conquest, Phaedrus also lost his name. In fact his very *existence* was entirely written out of the script by his medieval heirs. What disappeared along with this, besides, was all the high energy editorializing that had marked out his *Fables* as a distinctive body of work. He had wanted to come across as himself something of a writer, and performer. Lively prologues and postscripts were cut by his successors; so, too, the odd bits of satire and the bulk of the anecdotes. Only a few, usually straight down the track misogynistic, fables with human characters survived the medieval cull.

In his role of storyteller, Phaedrus had in fact determined to take an exceptionally high profile. He often throws himself into the "morals" that head or foot the fables. On occasion, he finds ways to break into the story itself, with asides, commentary, first-person "reaction." He links the fables, by signal or by innuendo, to his own situation in life: he "commandeers" the mask of *Aesop.* In the end, the storytelling voice even becomes an extra "character" in its own right. When the narrator does this, the intervention will be *italicized* in the stories. There it will be, this voice, waiting in the margins and between the lines, plotting surprise intrusions and intermittent raids (see notes on **1–2**, **41–42**).

All told, then, Phaedrus made a big pitch to wrest authority from the father figure Aesop. He meant to share the *Fables* with him, by dint of his own interventions, and mounted a bid for the status of coauthor (see **1**). The tales are indeed, overwhelmingly, of Greek origin, and so the "cultural property" of Aesop (see Tables for Fables for data, p. 127). And they were never likely to stay *Phaedrus's* fables. This is why *Aesop's Human Zoo* calls them "Roman stories": for "Phaedrus's zoo" it is not; yet the "Roman Aesop" has left his mark all over his ravaged legacy. We should respect both sides of this tale.

Phaedrus, then, missed out on his full share of eternity. His heyday was to come in seventeenth- and eighteenth-century salons and schools (see Further Reading). His little tales came into their own at that point because they are written in *Latin.* In easy colloquial verse, and easily mastered: hence our fifty texts appear with their translations. They have always made ideal early reading in class. But that's not all they have going for them. You will soon find that they take us on short trips down all manner of odd byways of ancient thinking, lore, and life. To drop in on social types familiar and bizarre, funny twists, strange proverbs, awful puns, touches of folklore, and saucy naughtiness: see Tempting Topics for zoo guide, p. 135. And, since these fables have their sights set on us all, if you're anxious to see if and where *you* are in the book, do consult The Cast of Characters, p. 131.

This was entertainment for Romans at the superpower peak of their empire, a spot of off-duty lightheartedness, in neat and on-the-button Roman style. Phaedrus knows exactly the sort of readers he wants us to be—sharp and jocular, reflective but relaxed. He lets us know he makes a great "Aesop" figure, as a former slave himself. All his stories tie human nature to the physical facts. They show just what can happen if we forget what we are made of.

It is a surefire recipe for humor, and our chance to hear Latin laugh.

Aesop's Fables and Every Body's

Whether or not the characters are animals, Aesop's fables are about the human condition. We depend so much on the daft fictions of our lexicon of animal metaphors. How many truths we tell (about) ourselves with all our daft talk with Ape Ass Beaver Bitch Bitch Bull Dog Fox Goat Hound Kid Lamb Lion Mouse Ox Snake Sow Stag Wasp Wolf (see Cast of Characters). *We* made the law of the jungle, stocked with beasts and brutes. That is what makes us shiver when the occasional story butts in to palm off a magic quirk of animal behavior, "for real," rather than fixing up a fable (see **33**, **39**).

Talk is what Fables are all about. Phaedrus is particularly clear about this. He very rarely lets a tale go by without making it talk. Usually the characters do it, but if they won't, he'll get into the act himself, as chatty, even voluble, narrator. When he does this, he acts out as writer what Aesop the street sage from the bottom of the social heap is pictured doing, "for real," in the myth of Fable. That is where the whole idea of fables is supposed to have come from. No fabulist can be caught speaking out against oppressors, since an Aesop's targets are dumb beasts. Dumb insolence is a tough nut to crack down on. Punishment would involve an element of self-accusation.

Phaedrus puts Aesop onto the page as "internal narrator."

This way, Phaedrus can tell us of the telling of a tale (**44**, seer talking to Father, as if Farmer to Ox). And Phaedrus puts Aesop into the story, so that he can make like one of his animals (**10** and **14**, trouncing experts) or so that we can drop by on a typical day in the life of the quick-tongued slave (**24**) or hear him "answer" questions on the mysteries of our lives, and our bodies (**8–9**). Phaedrus likes to make the voices play, so that Lamb lectures (**7**), while Venus gives Hen the third degree, in order to make Juno laugh (**12**)—but I shan't give away any more here. You'll see.

Most analyses of the world, or nature, of Fable focus on general attitude, or "ideology." Sardonic about shame and cruel about cruelty, Fable mocks pretensions and pricks vanity, to remind us all of our own limitations. Penalties can be harsh, mistakes fatal and insult mortifying. . . . The way we might imagine that slaves would tell slaves about slavery. Utterly different from our humane lives as humans. Yet not so very different, after all. Since we are all slaves in some respects.

Thus, it's true that Fable shows how self-mockery can inoculate against insult as well as injury. And shows, too, that mockery can pose as self-mockery. No slave need ever be motivated by solidarity with any other slave. There isn't any reason why slaves should stick together or trust one another, any more than any other social relation. There is always "slippage," tension, suspicion, treachery in any bond. And it was in the interests of owners to make sure that dissension ruled the lives of their slaves. There is a linked point about Fable that I should like to bring to your attention before we go any further.

The conversation that passes between Phaedrus's animals, people, gods, and trees is saturated with Latin buzzwords of politeness, business, friendship, kinship, compliment, complaint. (See the huge entry under "Social Relations" in Tempting Topics). The *talk* that Phaedrus makes one and all of his creatures and people talk is, naturally, implanted in imaginary scenarios of social inter*action.* For when *Aesop's Fables* come to Rome, they present a long parade of characters who are bound to "act out" all the basic roles of Phaedrus's community. This makes Fable a good place to look for the rules creating Romanness. An imperial *Human Zoo.*

But, and so, there is plenty of plain silliness, and cheerful fun, too, in this menagerie of Man and manners. Whenever the body claims due respect from us, there's a smile and a jolt waiting round the corner. Fable knows, perfectly well, that our bodies (don't) make us us.

So let me just make one further polished, ridiculous, true remark here (~ **1**). It is about the point of the headings I shall use to group the stories. I do mean to tie storytelling in close to humanity. There is plenty to think about in a set of simple claims we can make about Fable. It is creative: fables imagine creation, and creativity. Fables are born: and birth is always a crisis (~ **2**–**7**). Fables pose as public speech. They are gendered. Of course they are gendered. They are part of male joking-behavior, what has been called "phallic brag." They wave misogyny in your face and know that's entertainment. On the other hand, naturally, they are about botchery, drunkenness. And so they make slips and spill secrets.

Fables impersonate females, as well as pontificating about them. And they undermine their own ability to do either (~ **8**–**12**). They are also tiny. They belong to the undersized, unassertive, ungrown; and should know it (~ **13**–**20**). Fables look unprepossessing, unattractive, unimposing, unimpressive. But they are parables, with beautiful truths locked up within. Fables are tales told, and telling them uses the voice. The voice obliges the storyteller to inhabit roles, to ventriloquize ways of being, and to commit to a view—one view among views (~ **21**–**27**).

Fables work on the human body piecemeal. They take us

apart, top and tail. They are themselves a fragile form of wisdom, all talking head and brash face (~ **28–30**). They *are* low-down culture, "crap" coming out of one orifice or another (~ **31–35**). Stories smear real audiences as they tell of fictional smears (~ **50**).

Fables come separately, but Fables also operate as a genre. They cancel and undermine each other, but they presuppose and rely on their like. This is an absolutely fundamental fix for a Fable *collection,* for a *book.* You will notice how I have disrespected Phaedrus's ordering of his collection, just like everyone else down the chain of transmission. But see how I have made a new ordering narrate an overall parable, a fable of Fable (~ **36–40**).

Finally, fables exercise power. They are linked in to the structures of social power, like all forms of narration. They frame as well as expose authority. They achieve targets by passing themselves off as old stuff. They pretend they belong to an old, old tradition, which once belonged to some other old fogy/respected Elder—Aesop. No, they do not die; they pass on (~ **41–49**).

A Human Zoo

All readers who enjoy reading stories can get into *these.* No prior knowledge of Roman culture, let alone classical Latin, is actually needed: but if you once learned some of the language, or if you feel like making a start, we are bringing you the original text, in parallel with my English translations. I don't think there's anything terribly decadent or obscene here, certainly not a single *gladiator* in sight. The stories are naughty enough to interest children like us, but harmless enough to show all the family, and join in. Light reading from Classical civilization is not, shall we say, abundant, so these neglected ancient tales have a certain paradoxical "novelty" value. Just be ready to surprise yourself, and find you are amused—and caught.

Tables for the Fables will tell exactly where the stories come from. You will find that *Aesop's Human Zoo* features several of the old favorites, as well as many animal fables you won't know.

Thirty-six of the fifty in the book are Phaedrian tales not found anywhere in Greek *Aesop*s. Thirty-one are first extant in Phaedrus and five in those medieval derivatives I told you about.

The other dozen stories do turn up in Greek, but usually in decidedly different variations. Eleven turn up in *Aesop*s. (See my note on **16**.) The oddments out are the editorial piece **1** and the harangue **2** (but see note on **2**).

People perform and suffer in many of these tales, whether ordinary types or off-beats, making wry comments and daft jokes on us all. The range of story types is wider than you could imagine, including fairy tale, quirks of beastlore, folklore, and superstition, a parable or two, and mock creation legends. Most of these tales have been good as forgotten, and they certainly are not to be found in other modern *Aesops*—before *Aesop's Human Zoo.*

NOTE

The stories in *Aesop's Human Zoo* are referred to by plain number in bold: **1–50**.

Italics in the translations indicate that this part of a fable speaks its "moral," or is delivered in the "moralizing" voice of the writer, compiler, poet, presenter. (See further the note to **2**.)

CAPITALS *in the texts and translations* represent "titles" supplied by Bishop Perotti: he cut the "morals" he found in Phaedrus and recycled the ideas in these headings. (Again, see the note to **2**.)

There are a few handy abbreviations. For these, see the Key to Tables for the Fables, p. 127.

Aesop's Human Zoo

THE STORIES

Creation and Birth

2

ASK NO MORE THAN IS FAIR.

Had Nature shaped mankind under my direction,
it would have been far and away better endowed.
Yes, I would have bestowed on us every facility
that generous Fortune assigned each of the beasts.
The elephant's strength, and lion's spring;
crow's life span, grim bull's pride and joy;
and the flying horse, its calm docility.
Yet to Man would still belong Man's own thing. Wits.

Hmm. Jupiter king of gods laughs up his sleeve,
I bet. Grand strategy denied all that to Man.
Lest we grab the cosmic sceptre. Our presumption.

Wherefore, may we ever stay content
with our award from invincible Jupiter.

May we run out the years of our destined span,
nor try for more than mortal condition permits.

: : :

NON ESSE PLVS AEQVO PETENDVM

Arbitrio si Natura finxisset meo
genus mortale, longe foret instructius.
Nam cuncta nobis attribuisset commoda
quae cuique indulgens Fortuna animali dedit
—elephanti uires et leonis impetum,
cornicis aeuum, gloriam tauri trucis,
equi uelocis placidam mansuetudinem—
et adesset homini sua tamen sollertia.

Nimirum in caelo secum ridet Iuppiter,
haec qui negauit magno consilio homini
ne sceptrum mundi raperet nostra audacia.

Ergo contenti munere inuicti Iouis
fatalis annos decurramus temporis
nec plus conemur quam sinit mortalitas.

If Phaedrus ruled the world . . . : I thought we had better hear him hold forth at the outset. He uses the stuff of Greek sermonizing here (cf. AES. 240, 431, esp. 311). Notice that this is a first-person rant. It is just as if we are in the middle of reading a *Life of Phaedrus* rather than a "fable" (see notes on **18** and **49** for fables that are told in the course of the ancient Greek *Life of Aesop*).

Phaedrus plays around on this occasion with the voice of a "preacher." He moves from naughty dig to pious uplift. This fabulist is not content to give us just any blank moralist, so he skips round all the different tactics he can think of. He means to liven it up and catch us nodding, unawares, or catch us out. When I "hear" a part of a tale as coming from this "*Moralist,*" I shall make sure you notice, by printing it *in italics.*

In our very next story (**3**), the "moral" element will be invasive. It will also be creative, again, by pointing to a proverbial pun behind the fable. Then, in **4**, contrast the slammingly straight moral: Bishop Perotti tidies Phaedrus's original morals into "titles" (see **39** for divergence from Phaedrus) or (as here) makes up his own rubric. He does *plonk* (try **7**). That is why, when we come to **24**, I shall actually have the nerve to *sabotage* his title. Where we depend on Perotti, though, I must give his "titles": they are very likely to represent a rewrite of something Phaedrus had written that didn't suit Perotti's book. To mark these "titles" out, I shall print them IN CAPITALS.

There will be no more from me, I promise, on these strictures — the "morals."

3

ON TRUTH AND FICTION.

Once upon a time hero Prometheus played potter,
and populated the young world's generation.

Taking exquisite pains he had created Truth.
She would deliver justice among human beings.

Suddenly summoned by great Jupiter's angel,
he entrusted his workshop to the trickster Guile.
He'd just taken him into apprenticeship.

Fired with zeal, Guile shaped a likeness with looks to match.
One and the same height. Every limb fair copy.
Handy craft, given time and opportunity.
Now the marvelous mold was near completely set.
But the clay ran out on him for making the feet.

Maestro returned. Which caused young Guile to scurry.
In panic and fright. He sat in his proper place.

Prometheus marveled at the copyist's perfection.
Wanted it thought the Triumph of Art, but his own.

So he put the two casts in the oven side by side.
When they were fired, and the life spirit poured in,
off strode saint Truth, with her unassuming stride.
But the amputee image stuck fast in her tracks.

Then the fake likeness, a steal of a work of art,
was given the name "Fiction."

And when people say
"Fiction has no feet," I, too, readily agree.

: : :

DE VERITATE ET MENDACIO

Olim Prometheus saeculi figulus noui

cura subtili Veritatem fecerat
ut iura posset inter homines reddere.

Subito accersitus nuntio magni Iouis
commendat officinam fallaci Dolo
in disciplinam nuper quem receperat.

Hic studio accensus, facie simulacrum pari
una statura, simile et membris omnibus,
dum tempus habuit callida finxit manu.
quod prope iam totum mire cum positum foret
lutum ad faciendos illi defecit pedes.

Redit magister, quo festinanter Dolus
metu turbatus in suo sedit loco.

Mirans Prometheus tantam similitudinem
propriae uideri uoluit artis gloriam.

Igitur fornaci pariter duo signa intulit.
Quibus percoctis atque infuso spiritu,
modesto gressu sancta incessit Veritas.
At trunca species haesit in uestigio.

Tunc falsa imago atque operis furtiui labor
Mendacium appellatum est

—quod negantibus
pedes habere facile et ipse assentio.

The "moral" points out the concept—or "pun-cept"—behind the fable. For, in Greek, there is a single word, *a-pous,* which means both "lacking feet" and "having no use of feet." Truth must stand firm, stand proud, stand tall—or there goes stability.

This story's visit to the artist's workshop, its craft techniques and personal dynamics, beats most (data for) "Art History" hollow. It footnotes a world of creativity that we can hardly ever glimpse.

Can a storyteller mean to tell us fiction is footloose and footling, and expect this to stand up? You will find, if you turn back to **1** for a reminder, that fiction is here casting truth as the work of fictional truth, and vice versa. Yes, this is a Fable.

4

No one likes moving back
to a place that has hurt them.

Birth is near, the pressure is on.
The months are all done.

The Woman was lying on the ground.
She was heaving, sobbing, groans.

Her man urged her, get yourself to bed.
A far better place to drop Nature's load.

"No way," she said, "do I trust the trouble can end
in the very place it was conceived at the start."

: : :

Nemo libenter recolit qui laesit locum.

Inſtante partu mulier actis mensibus
humi iacebat flebilis gemitus ciens.

Vir eſt hortatus, corpus lecto reciperet,
onus Naturae melius quo deponeret.

"Minime," inquit, "illo posse confido loco
malum finiri quo conceptum eſt initium."

Is the woman silly? Is she instructive? Obviously right? Superstitiously abandoning father's bed for mother earth?

Is this throwback folklore, or female protest leaking through male mockery? Does the story "work" because we are bound to "hear" it differently?

I believe it is, and we are.

The scenario of birth delivers the word, and idea, of "Nature"—which is posh Latin for "womb"—a heavily "natal" nuance (*natura*). This can give the woman still more right to tell us all.

5

It's a trap:
sweet-talking rogue.
Pass it by.
Moral verses below:

Bitch was whelping, asked another
for her home to drop the litter.

Got an easy yes. The home was reclaimed:
she turned to pleas. "Just a short while, OK.

Till she can convoy strong enough pups."

Used up that while too. The campaign begins
to hot up, for the return of the rooms.

"If you can take on both me and my clutch,"
she says, "then sure I'll give up on the place."

: : :

Habet insidias hominis blanditiae mali.
Quas ut uitemus uersus subiecti monent.

Canis parturiens cum rogasset alteram,
ut fetum in eius tugurio deponeret,

facile impetrauit. Dein reposcenti locum
preces admouit, tempus exorans breue,

dum firmiores posset catulos ducere.

Hoc quoque consumpto flagitari ualidius
cubile coepit.

"Si mihi et turbae meae
par," inquit, "esse potueris, cedam loco."

Phaedrus felt like putting **5** next to **4**, so he did. I think it's easy to feel what this says about humans and their zoo.

The Middle Ages versions cut the Humans but kept the Bitches (and the Sow of **6**).

6

ESSENTIAL: TO TRY A PERSON OUT BEFORE YOU TRUST YOURSELF TO THEIR GOOD FAITH.

Birth is due. The push is on.
Sow flat out. Starts up to moan.

Dashing over, Wolf. Says, he can serve
the midwife role; promises help.

She truly knew the bad heart's sham.
Rejects a rogue's dodgy kindness.

Says, "That's fine, just you keep well away."

There now, if she had trusted herself to Wolf's bad faith,
she'd have cried at her death in the same pain as at birth.

: : :

FACIENDVM PRIVS DE HOMINE PERICVLVM QVAM EIVS TE COMMITTAS FIDEI

Premente partu scrofa cum gemeret iacens,

accurrit lupus et obstetricis partibus
se posse fungi dixit, promittens opem.

Quae uero nosset pectoris fraudem improbi,
suspectum officium repudiauit malefici

et "Satis est," inquit, "si recedis longius."

Quodsi perfidiae se commisisset lupi,
pari dolore fata deflesset sua.

The "moral" makes the point. Birth must always be a life and death crisis.

Look! Another *fable* is born, for *Aesop's Human Zoo.*

Our next story will pull the wool from our eyes, with a lamb's-eye view on life. Lamb is going to prize the social relation of parenting above physical maternity. It can read as a remarkably advanced take on nurture above nature.

But hasn't that Dog always been *right?*

7

Lamb is astray among the nanny goats. Dog said:
"Fool, you're in the wrong place. Your mother is not here."
He pointed where the ewes were penned off. Far away.

"I don't want the one impregnated when she pleased,
who carried the unknown burden for months to term,
ultimately dropping the baggage that slipped out.
I want the one that brought her teats close to feed me,
cheating her offspring of milk to have plenty for me."

"But the one who bore you must come first."

"No, not so.
How did she know if I would be born black or white?
Furthermore. Had she wanted to bear a female,

what good would that have been—I was delivered male?
A great favor she did me, on my day of birth,
sure she did, to wait for the butcher by the hour.

Her control of the process that made me was zilch.
'Must come first'? Not she who pitied a helpless babe
—who volunteers the sweet fostering she provides?

Generosity, not genetics, makes parents."

The fabulist intended his verse as a proof:
People defy laws. They surrender to love.

: : :

Inter capellas agno palanti canis
"Stulte," inquit, "erras; non eſt hic mater tua,"
ouesque segregatas oſtendit procul.

"Non illam quaero quae cum libitum eſt concipit,
dein portat onus ignotum certis mensibus,
nouissime prolapsam effudit sarcinam,
uerum illam quae me nutrit admoto ubere,
fraudatque natos lacte ne desit mihi."

"Tamen illa eſt potior quae te peperit."

"Non ita.

unde illa sciuit niger an albus nascerer?
Age porro, parere si uoluisset feminam,
quid profecisset cum crearer masculus?
Beneficium sane magnum natali dedit,
ut expectarem lanium in horas singulas.

Cuius poteſtas nulla in gignendo fuit,
cur hac sit potior quae iacentis miserita eſt,
dulcemque sponte praeſtat beneuolentiam?

Facit parentes bonitas, non necessitas."

His demonſtrare uoluit auctor uersibus
obsiſtere homines legibus, meritis capi.

S · x and Gender

8 *and* 9

*   *   *   *   *   *   *   *

*   *   *   *   *   *   *   *

*   *   *   *   *   *   *   *

*   *   *   *   *   *   *   *

*   *   *   *   *   *   *   *

. . . woman's tongue, by molding on a male organ.

That's where perversion derived the homology.

[9]

A second question. What brought lesbians and male effeminates into the world? Old-un said it all:

"Prometheus again. Creator of our clay mob
which shatters at once on any bump into Fortune.

He had spent all day in fashioning one by one
the natural parts which decency hides with clothes.
Next he could go and fit them onto their torsoes.

Came a call to dinner from the free god Bacchus.
There he sluiced out his veins with plenty of nectar.
And then returned home late, tottery on his feet.

With his brain half-asleep, he made a sozzled slip.
He fitted the part of a girl to the male sex,
and he fitted the parts of males onto females."

So now lust enjoys the pleasures of perversion.

: : :

* * * * * * * *

* * * * * * * *

* * * * * * * *

* * * * * * * *

* * * * * * * *

. . . affictione ueretri linguam mulieris.

Affinitatem traxit inde obscenitas.

[9]

Rogauit alter, tribadas et molles mares
quae ratio procreasset. exposuit senex:

"Idem Prometheus, auctor uulgi fictilis
qui simul offendit ad fortunam frangitur,

naturae partes ueste quas celat pudor
cum separatim toto finxisset die,
aptare mox ut posset corporibus suis,

ad cenam est inuitatus subito a Libero.
Vbi irrigatus multo uenas nectare
sero domum est reuersus titubanti pede;

tum semisomno corde et errore ebrio
applicuit uirginale generi masculo
et masculina membra applicuit feminis.

Ita nunc libido prauo fruitur gaudio."

I won't do this to you again. I did say poor Phaedrus's work comes down in tatters.

Did monks find the filth hereabouts too hot to handle? It looks obvious—but the previous two tales in Phaedrus (4.13–14) are in the same sort of mess, and they aren't *sexually* obscene, if that is what we guess must have bothered medieval scribes (see my book listed in Further Reading).

What does it all mean? Well, Phaedrus has spliced this pair of fables together (unlike **4–5**). This lets us see from **9** that the almost completely lost **8** was also a lowdown "Creation story" (like **3**), and it, too, starred anatomical botchery from the same craftsman Prometheus. The "Old-un" will have been Aesop, and we must have just missed his first question.

So far as **8** goes, imagine what we have lost and risk a revelation, plus your reputation. Some say it was just (just!) about Women sticking out their tongues, pretending that they must have been issued with penises, for one reason or another, when the body parts were dished out. Poor girls! Penis envy, or what?

But the rest of us cannot repress the thought that too much here smacks of sexual engineering. Surely "Woman's tongue" was "mould[ed] on," precisely, as substitute phallus? Is oral sex the story, and hot talk of the mechanics of lesbian action? Lucky girls?

Does the *bad* joke leak an erotic secret—do you think that this was actually the *right* place to put it?

Everything essential is in place in **9**, and nowhere to hide. Prometheus screws up some more. His name is Greek and spells "Forethought." He is *not* managing to live up to it.

According to these tales, or my version of them, at any rate, sexual misfits are bonus party fun. And the aftereffects of alcohol live up to Bacchus, the "Liberator." That is the name he is given here: *Liber.* And it is the right name, too.

Let's try a more aggressively analytic approach for a moment and take a hard look at the structure of these tales. If sexual deviance is told as inversion of normalcy, then binary symmetry must map the *other* combinations of genitalia onto the logic of our bodies. Miscreant "active" women and "passive" men *must* have been part of (mis)creation. Calling Prometheus half-cut and half-asleep, out of control and offtrack, means that his *other* half must have been . . . inspired and awake, experimenting and pioneering.

Maybe these eloquent, torn fragments do have much more to tell us than mere homophobias?

10

Experience teaches more truth than a crystal ball.
So the popular saying holds. But no one tells why.
This will become lore, thanks to this fable of mine.

Someone kept Sheep. His ewes had lambs.
But with human heads. Omen. Scare.
Scurried to consult the seers. Gloom.

One saw it heading for master:
"Sacrifice, fend off the peril!"

One's sure that wife must be cheating.
"The children are bastards, it meant:
You'll atone with a bigger beast!"

Why dilate? Verdicts clash, at odds.
Load the man's cares with bigger cares.

There Aesop stood. Old nose quite clean.
Nature could never tell him tales:

"So. To curate your portent, squire,
get," he said, "wives for your shepherds."

: : :

Vsu peritus hariolo ueracior
uulgo esse fertur, causa sed non dicitur.
Notescet quae nunc primum fabella mea.

Habenti cuidam pecora pepererunt oues
agnos humano capite. monstro exterritus
ad consulendos currit maerens hariolos.

Hic pertinere ad domini respondet caput
et auertendum uictima periculum,

ille autem affirmat coniugem esse adulteram
et insitiuos significari liberos
sed expiari posse maiore hostia.

Quid multa? uariis dissident sententiis
hominisque curam cura maiore aggrauant.

Aesopus ibi stans naris emunctae senex
Natura numquam uerba cui potuit dare:

"Si procurare uis ostentum, rustice,
uxores," inquit, "da tuis pastoribus."

II

Nanny Goats were granted
beards by Jupiter.

Billy Goats were dismayed
and began to complain,
"Females. Equalizing
the honor that is ours."

Jupiter said, "Leave them be.
Let them joy in empty pomp,
take on trappings of your job.
So long as they don't match
the courage that is yours."

This story's moral:
Put up with people
who are like you in image
but are no match in valor.

: : :

Barbam capellae cum impetrassent ab Ioue,

hirci maerentes indignari coeperunt
quod dignitatem feminae aequassent suam.

"Sinite," inquit, "illas gloria uana frui
et usurpare ueſtri ornatum muneris,
pares dum non sint ueſtrae fortitudini."

Hoc argumentum monet ut suſtineas tibi
habitu esse similes qui sunt uirtute impares.

12

WOMEN . . . AND LUST.

Juno, queen of marriage, had hymned
Juno's self-control in sex.

Live, to gods and goddesses,
insistently she swore:
mating is best arranged,
when females wed *one* male.

Venus, queen of love, did not demur.
She went looking for the fun.

To clinch that Juno has no like
(they say) she quizzed a Hen like this:

"Please say. How much to eat's OK?"

Hen's answer was: "Whatever
you give. Sure to be OK.
If, that is, you let my feet
go scratch me up something else."

"To *not* scratch—is a sack of corn OK?"

"Sure. Too much. And yet—do let me scratch."

"To *not* scratch, not even once—what price?"

The end. Hen owned up to nature's flaw,

"Allow me the run of a silo—and
I shall be scratching just the same."

Juno, they say, laughed. At Venus's joke.

In Hen, she satirized all Females.

: : :

Cum castitatem Iuno laudaret suam,

dis et deabus asserens praesentibus
mari coniungi melius uni feminam,

iucunditatis causam haud depellit Venus,

nullamque ut affirmaret esse illi parem,
interrogasse sic gallinam dicitur:

"Dic sodes quanto possis satiari cibo."

Respondit illa, "Quicquid dederis, satis erit,
sic ut concedas pedibus aliquid scalpere."

"Ne scalpas," inquit, "satis est modius tritici?"

"Plane, immo nimium est, sed permitte scalpere."

"Ex toto, nequid scalpas, quid desideras?"

Tum denique illa fassa est Naturae malum:

"Licet horreum mi pateat, ego scalpam tamen."

Risisse Iuno dicitur Veneris iocos,

quia per gallinam denotarit feminas.

"A hen scratches," declared a Greek proverb—like that limerick on the Young Lady from Natchez: "When aah itches, aah scratches." Socrates can explain: "Tell me, if someone with an itch who scratches, can scratch without restraint, and spends life scratching, will live happily . . . —Not just pleasantly, but also happily? . . . As long as he scratches only his head, . . . or must I ask you still more?" (Plato, *Gorgias* 494c–3). The fable immortalizes "prurience" (from the Latin for *itch*), constructing woman as automaton: yes, it declares, a hen is programmed for stimulus-response; but her reflex is wired in as default mechanism. So don't ask "What does Woman want?," but know that "Woman w a n t s."

Isn't this [fable] what *men* want? (English "wanton" is folk-etymologized from "want.")

By the way, the second and third lines of **12** are taken from the medieval paraphrases. They are missing from the Phaedrus manuscripts.

Size and Shape

13

A nobody makes like somebody big.
He's dead.

Once upon a meadow
Frog caught sight of Ox.

She was hit by jealousy.
How can it be that big?

She puffed up her wrinkly skin. Asked
her spawn, am I broader than Ox?
"No."

She strained her skin again. A
much bigger heave. Same query, though.
Who's bigger, who?

"Ox," the reply.

Finally infuriated,

she meant to puff up still more
pneumatically, but then
her body burst. There. She lay flat.

: : :

Inops, potentem dum uult imitari, perit.

In prato quondam rana conspexit bouem
et tacta inuidia tantae magnitudinis

rugosam inflauit pellem: tum natos suos
interrogauit, an boue esset latior.
Illi negarunt.

Rursus intendit cutem
maiore nisu et simili quaesiuit modo,
quis maior esset.

Illi dixerunt bouem.

Nouissime indignata dum uult ualidius
inflare sese, rupto iacuit corpore.

14

HOW CHUCKING WEIGHT AROUND GETS SQUASHED. SOMETIMES.

What happened? When a Winner
in famous Athletic Games
was chucking his weight around.

Aesop saw. That Maharishi
asked, had his opponent been
the stronger man? "Say no such thing.
My strength was superior by far."

"Then, fool," he said, "what glory
did you earn? If you the stronger
defeated the weaker man?
We would have had to stand it
if you said you won on skill,
beat someone better off in strength."

: : :

QVOMODO COMPRIMATVR ALIQVANDO IACTANTIA

Victorem forte gymnici certaminis
iactantiorem cum uidisset Phryx sophus,

interrogauit an plus aduersarius
ualuisset eius. Ille: "Ne istud dixeris,
multo fuere uires maiores meae."

"Quod," inquit, "ergo, stulte, meruisti decus,
minus ualentem si uicisti fortior?
Ferendus esses, arte si te diceres
superasse, melior qui fuisset uiribus."

15

Gnat challenged Bull,
to a trial of strength.

Each and every nation
came to watch the show.

Then said puny Gnat:
"That's quite enough for me.
You turned up, to duel.
I'm already your match,
on your own reckoning."

He took off on the breeze
light as his wings.

He mocked the crowds.
Left Bull's threats behind.

If Bull had not forgot
the power of his neck,
he would have scorned
a humiliating foe.

Not made himself a butt
for unbecoming brag.

How to lower your reputation.
Bracket yourself with inferiors.

: : :

Culex cum taurum prouocasset uiribus,
uenerunt populi cuncti, ut spectacula cernerent.

Tunc paruus culex,
"Satis," inquit, "habeo quod conuenisti comminus.
Par tibi factus sum iudicio tuo."

Hic se per auras sustulit penna leui

lusitque turbam et tauri destituit minas.

Quodsi fuisset ualidae ceruicis memor,
pudendum contempsisset inimicum,

ineptae materia nec fuisset gloriae.

Quia ille sibi famam diminuit, qui se indignis comparat.

See Phaedrus go, clambering all over this fable!
His "Gnat" became the Middle Ages' "Flea": in Latin, *pulex* for *culex.* Big deal.

16

Do no one harm.
Retaliate in kind.
Fable says so—
That's the moral.

Fox in the tale told with Stork.

Took the lead with a dinner date.
On his plate, served up no-solids
soup. No way could famished Stork
get a bite. By return over went Fox.

Servings were ensconced in a jar.
She stuck in her beak, and filled herself up.
Her dinner guest she tortured with hunger.
Licking the jar's neck, he had no success.

That exotic bird said, I've heard tell:
"Be done by as you've done. Fair's fair."

: : :

Nulli nocendum: siquis uero laeserit,
multandum simili iure fabella admonet.

Ad cenam uulpes dicitur ciconiam

prior inuitasse et illi in patina liquidam
posuisse sorbitionem, quam nullo modo
guſtare esuriens potuerit ciconia.
Quae uulpem cum reuocasset, intrito cibo
plenam lagoenam posuit: huic roſtrum inserens
satiatur ipsa et torquet conuiuam fame.
Quae cum lagoenae collum fruſtra lamberet,

peregrinam sic locutam uolucrem accepimus:
"Sua quisque exempla debet aequo animo pati."

The Greek essayist Plutarch must have found this in an *Aesop:* it must be accident that none of *our* Aesop collections have it.

This is the fable that no dinner party can possibly do without.

17

"WHEN THE LIONSKIN FALLS SHORT GET YOURSELF STITCHED IN A FOX'S." MEANING: WHEN BODY STRENGTH FALLS SHORT, SEE YOU MAKE USE OF CUNNING.

What luck! Snake seized Lizard,
facing the other way.

Meant to swallow, down
the yawning gullet.

Liz grabbed what was in reach.
A twig, there on the ground.

Bit fast, in crosswise grip.
Curbed the jaws' anticipation
with this bar of inspiration.

Snake let go his mouth:
the catch had been in vain.

: : :

VBI LEONIS PELLIS DEFICIT, VVLPINAM INSVENDVM ESSE: HOC EST, VBI DEFICIVNT VIRES, ASTV VTENDVM

Serpens lacertam forte auersam prenderat,

quam deuorare patula cum uellet gula,

arripuit illa prope iacentem surculum,

et pertinaci morsu transuersum tenens,
auidum sollerti rictum frenauit mora.

Praedam dimisit ore serpens irritam.

Just so. This story gets hold of a primal body logic of confrontation.

One bite of exotic Greek lore has the same thing, but with Chameleon foiling Snake. I'm told that a Sanskrit Crane plugs a Sanskrit Lion.

Kipling's Mariner, "a person of infinite-resource-and-sagacity," improvised his block on annihilation with braces (on no account forget the braces, o best beloved) and bits of raft. He was getting swallowed by the Whale.

Tintin, and Captain Ketchup, when the time comes, use a rifle, and a telescope, to thwart their respective crocs.

Just so every other cartoon.

18

To cross the river an easy way,
Mouse asked Frog to help.

With a cord she tied together
her back leg, Mouse's front foot.

So they swam their swim.
And reached midstream.

Frog broke faith, and dived.
Dragged down Mouse,
with him beneath the water.

The corpse floated.
Bobbing in the ripples.

A hawk in flight
sighted prey.

Grabbed Mouse,
whipped off his
companion,
Frog.

> *Faithlessness. Schemed*
> *against another's life.*
> *Met death alongside.*
>
> *Self-inflicted vengeance.*
>
> *Harm others, and die.*

: : :

Mus quo transire posset facile flumen,
petiit ranae auxilium.

Illa poſteriori cruri suo lino alligat pedem priorem muris.

Natantes uenerunt in medium amnem.

Mutata fide submersit se rana,
et traxit secum sub aquas soricem.

Quem mortuum, surgens cum fluctuaret,

conspexit praedam miluus uolans,

mure rapto comitemque ranam abstulit.

Perfida quae de salute alterius aduersa cogitat,
experta simul exitium et ipsa consumpta est.

Qui nocent aliis interimunt.

Aesop tells this tale at the end of his *Life* (§133), which is a spoof biographical novel in ancient Greek. There, he is defying the holy Greek city of Delphi in court. Framed and condemned, he will be thrown over a cliff. And that is the end of him. Well, no, in some ways that's *not* the end.

You can also find the fable on the Bayeux Tapestry. In the margin.

Real mice seem to be able to swim. Well, most of them.

19

VILLAINS ARE NOT TO BE TRUSTED.

A Bird—*known in the country as "Groundling,"*
because, for sure, it makes its nest on the ground—
chanced to meet a bad Vixen.

On sight, she lifted high,
high on her wings.

"Greetings," went the other,
"Why shun me? I must know.
    As if food to spare isn't there,
    out in the field for me:
        crickets and beetles,
        locusts in a plague . . .
    There is no call for your fear.
    I dearly love you lots.
For your placid nature,
for your virtuous life."

Back came the reply:
                                        "Bravo.
A fine overture from you.
    On the plain I am not,
        up in the sky I am,
            a perfect match for you.
                So follow, do. And then, and
                    so, I trust my life to you."

: : :

PRAVIS NON ESSE FIDEM ADHIBENDAM

    Auis quam dicunt "terraneolam" ruſtici,
    in terra nidum quia componit scilicet,
forte occucurrit improbae uulpeculae,

qua uisa pennis altius se suſtulit.

"Salue," inquit illa, "cur me fugisti, obsecro?
Quasi non abunde sit mihi in prato cibus,
grilli, scarabaei, locustarum copia.
Nihil est quod metuas: ego te multum diligo
propter quietos mores et uitam probam."

Respondit contra:

"Tu quidem bene praedicas.
In campo non sum, sed par sub diuo tibi.
Quin sequere: salutem tibi sic committo meam."

The Latin word for this bird, *terraneola,* you won't find in the dictionaries. I suspect it can be found only here. It's a Roman touch from Phaedrus.

But it "grounds" the logic of the fable, too.
There is earth, and there is sky.
Can Vixen talk her way up to join the birds?
From foxhole to outer space.

20

The Birds were at war with the Beasts.
Now they were victorious.
Again they were vanquished.

Bat was more than afraid,
the outcome was never clear.

Soon as he saw one side on top,
he ferried himself off to them.

When peace returned as before,
the con was uncovered.
Obvious to both tribes.

So he was condemned.
The crime was that shameful,
he ran from the light.
Buried himself away
in dark, dark gloom.

Anyone who commits
themself to both camps
will spend their lifetime
unloved in both places,
awful in their own eyes.

: : :

Bellum gerebant uolucres cum quadrupedibus
et modo uincentes iterum uincebantur.

Vespertilio dubios euentus timens,
superiorem quam partem primo uidisset
ad eam se conferebat.

In pacem cum redissent pristinam
utrique generi fraus decepta apparuit.

Damnatus ergo tam pudendo crimine
lucem refugiens atris se condidit tenebris noctis.

Quia quisquis a duabus partibus se uindicari desiderat utrisque ingratus turpiter uiuit.

Ostrich plays the bats' part in a Greek version (AES. 418).

Bat is the only mammal capable of true flight.

You should know, at the end, that Greek calls the *Fledermaus* "night creature" (*nukteris*) and Latin calls it "evening creature" (*uespertilio*).

Sight and Sound

21

An actor's mask, the tragic kind.

Fox, it happened, saw the mask. Turned it
this way, then that way,
once and again.

"Pow," he cried, "what an impressive sight!
But no brain at all."

This saying is for the ones
handed honor and glory by Fortune
but likewise robbed of common sense.

: : :

Personam tragicam forte uulpes uiderat:

quam poſtquam huc illuc semel atque iterum uerterat

"O quanta species," inquit, "cerebrum non habet."

Hoc illis dictum est quibus honorem et gloriam
Fortuna tribuit, sensum communem abstulit.

If this jest is about us, it "sees off" (shoos) any form of personality cult perfectly adequately (*persona* is Latin here for "mask"). If it dramatizes Fable, it insults the edifice of culture in tying "honor and glory" to a stage prop. But how superficial the jest. And where's the "common sense" in the insult? The more you "turn it, this way, then that," the less **21** will command assent. Its masquerade will even read best, eventually, as self-satirizing parody: Fable looks deep into Fable's brain and finds there's nothing there. Who needs a Fox to tell us that—when we have Shakespeare? Fable only works because this is how masks work: if *they* were clever, they would be no use to us, and we could not know who we are, clever or whatever. *That's* more like common sense. On show in numbskull fables designed to fox us.

The third verse is restored from the medieval paraphrases: "this way, then that way."

22

Someone saw an Ape. Hung up
for sale at the butcher's shop.
In with the other items.
All the stock and the treats.

Asked, "Is he saucy at all?"
At this the worthy butcher joked:
"Same quality, sauce and source."

This remark, I think, was said
more for the mirth than the truth.
I've often found the beauties are the worst.
I've known a lot of ugly mugs are the best.

: : :

Pendere ad lanium quidam uidit simium
inter relicuas merces atque opsonia,

quaesiuit quidnam saperet. Tum lanius iocans:
"Quale," inquit, "caput eſt, talis praeſtatur sapor."

Ridicule magis hoc dictum quam uere aeſtimo
quando et formosos saepe inueni pessimos
et turpi facie multos cognoui optimos.

"Sauce"? This is, truly, an unsavory story, as customer and butcher thuddingly pun on *sapor,* which means both "savor" and "sapience." Fable tells us, for once, that in this life you get what you see. Beware: Ape is as smart as he looks.

But (we ask) what is Ape supposed to be up to here? A cuddly pet in a cage, or monkeying around, swinging from carcass to joint? Or dead meat, hung up for sale and weighed by the pound? Buy now: Ape tastes as bad as he looks. Here is wisdom, in the marketplace.

Can the laughing butcher sell us any such . . . story?
Our source and our savior.
Phaedrus is having none of it.
We should shop around for fables.
He did. I have. And you are.

23

A warning for this warning:
Take a good look at yourself.
Make it part of your routine.

Someone with the ugliest daughter
and a specially good-looking son.

A mirror put on their mother's chair
they chanced to spot in a children's game.

He brags, "I'm Prince Charming." She sees red.
Won't have show-off brother making fun.
Takes it all, what else, as aimed her way.

She scoots off to Father to hit back.
With great malice incriminates son—
who touched women's gear, and him a *male*!

He hugs the pair. Gives a kiss to each.
Shares between them fond affection. Bids:
"Each day, I ask, you use the mirror.
You, not to spoil your looks being bad.
You, to trounce your looks by acting good."

: : :

Praecepto monitus saepe te considera.

Habebat quidam filiam turpissimam
idemque insignem pulchra facie filium.

Hi speculum in cathedra matris ut positum fuit
pueriliter ludentes forte inspexerunt,

hic se formosum iactat, illa irascitur
nec gloriantis sustinet fratris iocos.
Accipiens, quid enim?, cuncta in contumeliam.

Ergo ad patrem decurrit laesura inuicem
magnaque inuidia criminatur filium
uir natus quod rem feminarum tetigerit.

Amplexus ille utrumque et carpens oscula
dulcemque in ambos caritatem partiens:
"Cotidie," inquit, "speculo uos uti uolo,
tu formam ne corrumpas nequitiae malis,
tu faciem ut istam moribus uincas bonis."

24

HOW DOES IT HURT TO TELL THE TRUTH? OFTEN.

Aesop was the slave of a Hideous Woman.

She frittered all day in painting herself up.
Put on a gown and pearls, silver and gold.

Found no man to lay finger on her, still.

He said, "A word or two, if I may?" "Speak."
"In my view. You'll get anywhere you please
if you cash in your set of glamour gear."

"That good-looking to you, just as I come?"
"Naw. No money down, and your bed will get rest."

"Well, your back won't get rest," she came right back.
Ordered flogging for the tongue-wagging slave.

Soon, a silver armlet is bagged by a thief.
It hasn't shown up, word comes to the Woman.

Filled with rage, she gathers all round. Promises
lashings in overload, if they don't tell the truth.

"Menace the rest," he said, "you won't fool me, boss.
I was horsewhipped for telling the truth just now."

: : :

QUAM NOCEAT SAEPE VERUM DICERE

Aesopus turpi cum seruiret feminae

quae se expingendo totum intricaret diem,
uestem uniones aurum argentum sumeret,

nec inueniret digito qui se tangeret,

"Licetne paucis?," inquit. "Dicas." "Censeo
quiduis efficies cultum si deposueris."

"Adeone per me uideor tibi meliuscula?"
"Immo, nisi dederis sponda cessabit tua."

"At non cessabunt latera," respondit, "tua,"
et obiurgari iussit seruum garrulum.

Poﬆ paulo armillam tollit fur argenteam.
Eam non apparere ut dictum eﬆ mulieri,

furore plena uocat omnes et uerbera
proponit grauia, uerum si non dixerint.

"Aliis minare," inquit, "me non fallere, era
—flagris sum caesus, uerum quia dixi modo."

25

Vocal bravado with zero valor:
the combination fools strangers
but stirs derision from familiars.

Lion went to hunt, and took Ass along.

Hid him behind a bush, and told him
to scare beasts with unfamiliar cry.

He'd catch them on the run.

So Big Ears
of a sudden raised a full-strength roar.
Freaked creatures with the weird fantasy.
Stampede. Hit familiar escape routes.

The onslaught. Lion blitzes them with shock.

Once carnage spent, he then called out Ass.
Ordered him to hush.

Upstart spoke out
of turn: "Rate the input of my voice."

"Special," he said. "Had I not known your
heart and kind, I'd have run too in fear."

: : :

Virtutis expers, uerbis iactans gloriam,
ignotos fallit, notis est derisui.

Venari asello comite cum uellet leo,

contexit illum frutice et admonuit simul,
ut insueta uoce terreret feras,

fugientes ipse exciperet.

Hic auritulus
clamorem subito totis tollit uiribus
nouoque turbat bestias miraculo.
Quae dum pauentes exitus notos petunt,

leonis affliguntur horrendo impetu.

Qui postquam caede fessus est, asinum euocat
iubetque uocem premere.

Tunc ille insolens:
"Qualis uidetur opera tibi uocis meae?"

"Insignis," inquit, "sic ut, nisi nossem tuum
animum genusque, simili fugissem metu."

The Greek moral would, I think, do.
Perfectly well: "Boasts trigger mockery."

26

Nanny goat with a newborn Kid.
Wanted to go out to pasture.

Warned him, not to open the door,
many beasts tour livestock stalls.

Warned and went, off to the wood.

Wolf arrived, and he mimicked
mother's voice. Said, "Open up,
open for your full udders."

Kid heard the voice, and he said,
as he peeked out through a chink,
"I hear mother's voice, but you
are fake and my enemy.
Through mother's voice you scheme to

drink my blood and eat my flesh.
One who knows you feared to leave
on your account. She warned me."

Hear those parental instructions,
and hear yourself getting praised.

: : :

Capella cum esset recens feta
ad paſtum uellens ire in siluam

ignarum monuit haedum et mandauit
ne clauſtrum alii aperiret, quod multas feras
uenire sciret ad ſtabula pecorum.

Ita commonuit haedum et sic siluam petiuit.

Paulo poſt uenit lupus, uocem adsimulans matris,
"Aperi mihi," inquit, "precor, aperi plenis tuis uberibus."

At haedus per rimas aspiciens et auscultans
ait, "Vocem matris audio,
sed tu, inique, fallax ac inimicus es.
Sub matris uoce noſtrum quaeris
sanguinem bibere et carnes edere.
Sed monuit me quae te nouit
et me metuit te propter relinquere."

Praecepta parentum audire natorum semper laus eſt.

My unusually naughty translation cobbles together *everything* there is in the three medieval versions we have. To capture the full infancy flavor.

The hair on "Wolf's chinny-chin-chin" would take a few more centuries to grow into the *Seven Little Kids* of Grimms' fairy tales.

By then, *Three Little Pigs* had set up as rivals. Huffing and Puffing.

27

Peacock's complaint to Juno, queen of gods.

Who didn't grant her nightingale song.

He was idolized by all the birds.
She was jeered the moment noise came out.

Then to console her the goddess said:

"But you win on looks, you win on size.
Emerald sheen shimmers on your neck.
Your jewelled tail unfurls rainbow plumes."

"What good's dumb show, if my sound can't win?"

"Roles were cast you by the Fates' decree:
looks—you; strength—eagle; song—nightingale,
presage—raven; evil portent—crow.
All satisfied with their special gift.

Don't covet what isn't your given.
Or else mocked hopes will slump to complaint."

: : :

Pauo ad Iunonem uenit, indigne ferens

cantus luscinii quod sibi non tribuerit:

illum esse cunctis auibus admirabilem,
se derideri simul ac uocem miserit.

Tunc consolandi gratia dixit dea,

"Sed forma uincis, uincis magnitudine.
Nitor smaragdi collo praefulget tuo
pictisque plumis gemmeam caudam explicas."

"Quo mi," inquit, "mutam speciem, si uincor sono?"

"Fatorum arbitrio partes sunt uobis datae:
tibi forma, uires aquilae, luscinio melos,
augurium coruo, laeua cornici omina,
omnesque propriis sunt contentae dotibus.
Noli affectare quod tibi non datum,
delusa ne spes ad querelam reccidat."

Juno plants the crow's "evil portent" to load her conclusion with doom.

It works.

They all want ~~Brains~~ Wigs

Hair and Head

28

One way or another,
Men get stripped by Women,
loving or loved.
A lesson we learn from telling tales.

There was a Middle-Aged Someone.

He was in the clutches of a Woman.
No innocent, hiding years with glamour.
And his heart had been won by a Girl.
A beautiful Girl.

They did both want
to look a match for him.
They started taking turns
sorting through his hair.

There he was. Thinking
he was getting groomed

by the Women's attentions.
In no time, he was bald.

You see, the Girl
had plucked out gray hairs.
The Old Timer
had plucked out black.

Systematic,
from the roots.

: : :

A feminis utcumque spoliari uiros,
ament amentur, nempe exemplis discimus.

Aetatis mediae quendam mulier non rudis
tenebat annos celans elegantia
animosque eiusdem pulchra iuuenis ceperat.

Ambae uideri dum uolunt illi pares
capillos homini legere coepere inuicem.

Qui se putarat fingi cura mulierum
caluus repente factus est.

Nam funditus
canos puella, nigros anus euellerat.

Are you surprised to find this one another Greek fable? I still am.

One version has: "A bad match will screw up."

And another (wouldn't you know it?), by a poet: "Women are like the sea. They smile, then suffocate."

After the Middle Ages, the misogyny turned to berating the Middle-Aged Man. Sir Roger L'Estrange will fire off: "It was now cuckow time . . .".

The story knows that women have no middle age. Not as sex toys.

29

Baldhead made a find.
It was at a crossroad.
As it happened.
A comb.

Up came a second
character.
Likewise
less his hair.

He said, "Hey.
Share
and share
alike."

The first one
showed his prize,
together
with the comment:

"The Gods have smiled down.
But cruel Fate is mean.
The saying goes, what we found
was coal instead of gold."

When hope has made a fool of someone,
complaining is in order.

: : :

Inuenit caluus forte in triuio pectinem.

Accessit alter aeque defectus pilis,
"Eia," inquit, "in commune quodcumque est lucri."

Ostendit ille praedam et adiecit simul,

"Superum uoluntas fauit, sed fato inuido
carbonem, ut aiunt, pro thesauro inuenimus."

Quem spes delusit huic querela conuenit.

How do you get three Greek proverbs in one miniature tale?

Two up front: "Bald man finds comb." "Coal, not treasure."

One held back: "Share a find" ("Mercury, god of luck, is in common").

No, you cannot take things as you find them. Stories know better: the logic is perfect. Fitting moral to fable, misfitting comb-treasure to pate-coal: 1 + 1 = 0.

30

SAME AS **2** ABOVE.

Once upon a time,
there were two Women, with Mercury,
god of travellers, for their guest.
They gave him a stingy, shabby, stay.

One had a baby son in the cradle.
The other's trade was prostitution.

So, for a thank-you to match their service,
just as he was about to go,
just on his way out the door,
he said, "It's a god you see.
I shall grant you immediately
whatever it is you each make your wish."

Mother humbly asks to see her child grow a beard as soon as
may be.
Whore asks that anything she's touched shall not get away
from her.

Mercury takes wing.
The Women go back inside:

Lo and behold, baby gives it all he's got.
Wailing through his beard.

The prostitute laughed heartily at that!
It happened her nostrils filled
with water, the way they do.

Meaning to wipe it,
she therefore grabbed her nose in her hand.
Drew the thing out so long, it went all the way down to the ground.

By laughing at somebody else,
she ended up the one to laugh at.

: : :

DE EODEM ALIA FABVLA

Mercurium hospitio mulieres olim duae
illiberali et sordido receperant

quarum una in cunis paruum habebat filium,
quaestus placebat alteri meretricius.

Ergo ut referret gratiam officiis parem
abiturus et iam limen excedens ait,
"Deum uidetis. tribuam uobis protinus
quod quaeque optarit."

Mater suppliciter rogat
barbatum ut uideat natum quam primum suum,
moecha ut sequatur sese quicquid tetigerit.

Volat Mercurius, intro redeunt mulieres.

Barbatus infans ecce uagitus ciet.

Id forte meretrix cum rideret ualidius
nares replentur umore, ut fieri solet.

Emungere igitur se uolens prendit manu
traxitque ad terram nasi longitudinem

et aliam ridens ipsa ridenda extitit.

Those "Three Wishes" that go so wrong *can* be found in an *Aesop,* for the first time, when a medieval peasant couple free a mountain dwarf (AES. 668).

An "iron beak" plays the role of that "sausage on the end of the nose," as the three moves get back to square one.

Does anyone think Phaedrus has the edge?

Genitals and Behinds

31

Eunuch's day in court with someone real bad.

Filthy gibes, spiteful vilification,
and a lambasting for lost body parts.

"Take note," he replied. "My sole cause for alarm:
I'm flawed through my lack of testimonials.

But, fool, why denounce crime committed by Fortune?
What is it ultimately shames a person?
Bad treatment
they *deserved.*"

: : :

Eunuchus litigabat cum quodam improbo

qui super obscena dicta et petulans iurgium
damnum insectatus est amissi corporis.

"En," ait, "hoc unum eſt cur laborem ualidius,
integritatis teſtes quia desunt mihi.

Sed quid Fortunae, ſtulte, delictum arguis?
Id demum eſt homini turpe quod meruit pati."

Eunuchus was a loan word in Latin from Greek: "the one who holds the bed"—i.e., the slave set by a husband to guard a wife from intruder. From lover.

Testis in the fable, on the other hand, is a strictly Latin pun: "witness" and "testicle."

You could just about mock up a plausible Greek version, but perhaps this really is a bona-fide *Roman* story, for a change.

Not so much a story as an accident waiting to keep happening.

A modern "Handyman," I'm told, missed a good job when he misunderstood what the lady of the house meant when she said, "Now let me see your testimonials."

32

MANY WOULD LIVE IF FOR THEIR LIVES THEY WOULD MAKE LIGHT OF THEIR—UPS AND DOWNS.

Beaver can't always escape the hounds.

> *Logorrheic Greeks call him "Castor":*
> *they've pinned a god's name to a beast.*

And Greeks pride themselves
on their wealth of words?

Folklore holds that Beaver
will rip off his own balls.

Because it's for these,
he sees, he is hunted.

I wouldn't rule it out.
This may happen,
maybe a plan,
part of god's design.

The hunter, you see, once
he finds his quarry, drops
running their owner down.
He'll call off the hounds.

If only human beings could manage it.
To agree to do without what they have.
Then they would live safe for the future.
No one would set traps for a bare body.

: : :

MVLTI VIVERENT SI SALVTIS GRATIA PARVI FACERENT FORTVNAS

Canes effugere cum iam non possit fiber

—Graeci loquaces quem dixerunt "castorem"
et indiderunt bestiae nomen dei,
illi qui iactant se uerborum copia—

abripere morsu fertur testiculos sibi,
quia propter illos sentiat sese peti.

Diuina quod ratione fieri non negem.

Venator namque simul inuenit remedium,
omittit ipsum persequi et uocat canes.

Hoc si praestare possent homines, ut suo
uellent carere, tuti posthac uiuerent.
Haud quisquam insidias nudo faceret corpori.

Beast lore, surely, not Aesopic fable. All the rattling of sabres must clinch it. This *has* to be Phaedrus's doing.

—But no, there Beaver is, in the Greek *Aesop,* already biting off those "castory" glands, for all he is worth.

Phaedrus does leave his mark, however, when he makes that hit at Greek "logorrhea" (Greek for verbal runs), presupposing the proverb "The Greeks have a word for it." And wishes them the beast of luck.

33

STINGINESS IS . . . STINGINESS IS NOT GLADHANDING EVEN WHAT IS SURPLUS TO NEEDS.

Ape asked Fox for a bit of tail:
so for decency's sake he could
cover up those bare buttocks.

The meanie went like this back:
"It can get even longer than it is.
Still I shall trail it through mud and thorns,
sooner than share with you even the shortest bit."

: : :

AVARVM ETIAM QVOD SIBI SVPEREST NON LIBENTER DARE

Vulpem rogabat partem caudae simius,
contegere honeste posset ut nudas nates.

Cui sic maligna, "Longior fiat licet,
tamen illam citius per lutum et spinas traham,
quam paruam quamuis partem impertiar tibi."

34

Once upon a time,
the Dogs sent ambassadors to Jupiter.
To plead for better conditions in life.
"Rescue us from humans and their insults.
They give us bread strewn with bits of bran.
We appease hunger mainly with awful dung."

The ambassadors set off, at no great pace.
Their noses were busy tracking tidbits in the
manure heap, so they didn't respond when called.
In the end Mercury just about located them.
They were in a state as he fetched them along.
And then! Once they faced Almighty Jupiter,

in fright they shat the whole palace over.
They were launched on their way out, with bats.

But Mighty Jupiter said, no send-off for them.

The Dogs marvelled, no ambassadors had returned.
Guessed something awful had been done by their people.
Time went by. They ordered some others appointed.
Rumor betrayed the earlier ambassadors.
For fear the same sort of things might all happen again,
they . . . filled up the dogs' anuses, with perfume—
yes, lots of it.

Instructions are handed over.
Instant send-off.

So this lot make their way there.
They are granted immediate audience. Then
the Most Mighty Father of Gods took the throne.
He caused his thunderbolt to shake.
Everything commenced to shudder.
The dogs panicked, because the crash was sudden.
At once they . . . shat perfume—
all mixed up with their dirt.
One and all were shouting loud,
the outrage must be avenged.

Before punishment, Jupiter made this speech: "No
king should refuse to send off ambassadors.
Nor is it hard to fix punishment to crime.
No! You will have this reward, as my sentence:
I do not forbid them a send-off.
But I ordain their torture by hunger,

so they . . . may never fail at holding in—
the contents of their stomachs.
Now for those who sent such useless people as you.
Ne'er shall they escape those humans and their insults."

So it is now. Their descendants still await
their ambassadors.
When any of them . . . sees a new arrival—
he smells his behind.

[No moral there.]

: : :

Canes legatos olim misere ad Iouem
meliora uitae tempora oratum suae,
ut sese eriperet hominum contumeliis,
furfuribus sibi conspersum quod panem darent
fimoque turpi maxime explerent famem.

Profecti sunt legati non celeri pede.
Dum naribus scrutantur escam in stercore,
citati non respondent. uix tandem inuenit
eos Mercurius et turbatos attrahit.
Tum uero uultum magni ut uiderunt Iouis,
totam timentes concacarunt regiam.
Propulsi uero fustibus uadunt foras.

Vetat dimitti magnus ille Iuppiter.

Mirati sibi legatos non reuertier,
turpe aestimantes aliquid commissum a suis,
post aliquid tempus alios ascribi iubent.
Rumor legatos priores prodidit.

Timentes rursus aliquid ne simile accidat,
odore canibus anum, sed multo, replent.

Mandata dantur et dimittuntur statim.

Adeunt. Rogantes aditum continuo impetrant.
Consedit genitor tum deorum maximus
quassatque fulmen: tremere coepere omnia.
Canes confusi subitus quod fuerat fragor,
repente odorem mixtum cum merdis cacant.
Reclamant omnes uindicandam iniuriam.

Sic est locutus ante poenam Iuppiter,
"Legatos non est regis non dimittere,
nec est difficile poenas culpae imponere.
Sed hoc feretis pro iudicio praemium:
non ueto dimitti, uerum cruciari fame,
ne uentrem continere non possint suum.
Illi autem qui miserunt uos tam futiles
numquam carebunt hominis contumeliis."

Ita nunc legatos expectant et posteri
nouum et uenire qui uidet culum olfacit.

Would you believe it, a Greek proverb told "people with sore eyes to look up a dog's bottom"; and their expressive phrase decided when some particular thing must have come "out of a dog's bottom."

This is the right moment to consider Jacques Lacan's redolent / constipated teaching, that what holds back Dogs from matching Humans is their strong sense of smell.

35

What generally happens to fools
when they chase a cheap laugh?
They rip into others with their gross abuse.
They provoke a crisis, of harm to themselves.

Donkey ran into Boar.

“Greetings,” he said, “bro’.”

He was cross, refused the approach.
Asked why he’d want to lie that way.

Donkey then let down his penis.

“If you deny you are like me,
still this is just like your snout.”

Boar wanted to attack, on his mettle.
But he smothered his rage, and said:

“Revenge is easy for me.
But I don’t want the stain
of a nobody’s blood.”

: : :

Plerumque stulti risum dum captant leuem,
graui destringunt alios contumelia
et sibi nociuum concitant periculum.

Asellus apro cum fuisset obuius,

"Salue," inquit, "frater."

Ille indignans repudiat
officium et quaerit cur sic mentiri uelit.

Asinus demisso pene, "Similem si negas
tibi me esse, certe simile est hoc rostro tuo."

Aper cum uellet facere generosum impetum,

repressit iram et, "Facilis uindicta est mihi,
sed inquinari nolo ignauo sanguine."

Part and Whole

36

No one is worth anything without their own.
For example, the Parts of the Human Body—

—So the story about them goes.
Once upon a time Hands and Feet got
cross. They refused to give Stomach food.
"Every day it sits there
without a stroke of work,
getting well stuffed, at rest."
Hands and Feet refused to work.
"We're slaves no more," they said.

Stomach got hungry, grumbled real loud.
For a few days, they would give it nothing.
Stomach was starving, all the Limbs collapsed.
Then they did want to give Stomach food.
This was refused. It had now shut down all routes.
So Limbs and Stomach hurt together.
And they died.

A finger-wagging fable.
Be stupid, walk out on your own.
Then find out the real mug is you.

: : :

Nemo aliquid ualet sine suis,
ut partes corporis humani,
de quibus dicitur

indignatas esse manus et pedes,
et uentri cibum dare noluerunt,
eo quod sine ullo labore
quotidie expleretur sedens otiosus.
Vnde grauiter indignantes aduersus eum,
manus et pedes laborare noluerunt
et negauerunt seruitudinem.

Venter uero esuriens clamabat.
At illi per paucos dies nihil ei dare uoluerunt.
Ieuno autem uentre omnia membra lassescunt.
Postea uero cibum dare uolentibus
recusauit uenter, quia iam clauserat uias.
Sic membra et uenter simul lassa intereunt.

Illos admonet fabula:
qui suos stulte deserit, se potius decipi sciat.

In the Greek variant, Stomach shuts Feet up: "If I didn't process food, you couldn't carry me, or anything else" (AES. 130). No body dies.

37

Man made an axe.
Petitioned the Trees: give me a handle.
Made from whatever wood is tougher than tough.

The rest ordered Wild Olive, you make the gift.

Man took the handle, fastened it secure,
started on branches and mighty trunks.
All and everything he pleased.
Chopping away without a qualm.

Then Oak told Ash:
"We deserve to suffer, right enough.
Our enemy came, he asked for a handle.
We gave him one."

Do think first.
Don't help out your enemy.

: : :

Securis cum fuisset facta, postulabat homo arbores sibi manubrium dare de ligno, quod esset omnium firmissimum.

Oleastro iusserunt dare ceterae.

Sumpsit homo manubrium aptatum securi,
ramos et robora magna, omniaque quae uellet, indubiose coepit incidere.

Sicque quercus fraxino ait,

"Digne et iuſte patimur,
quae roganti hoſti noſtro manubrium dedimus."

Vt cogites ante ne hoſti aliqua praeſtes.

38

What you despised is more useful than what you admired.
It often proves to be, and this story is witness to that fact.

Stag at the spring. Drank, paused,
saw his reflection in the water.

There he was, wowed.
Admired those "*branching* antlers."
The legs he bawled out—
"slenderness *to a fault.*"

Suddenly, hunters.
Scared at their voices,
he started to bolt for it.

Across the plain.
Fleet running foiled the hounds.

Then the forest harbored the creature.
The antlers caught in it, he was tangled fast.

He started getting torn.
Savage bites from the hounds.

Now he is dying, so it is said,
these are the words he uttered:

"Cry for me, luckless me.
At the end, now I understand.
How useful to me were what I scorned.
What I admired, how much grief they brought."

: : :

Laudatis utiliora quae contempseris
saepe inueniri testis haec narratio est.

Ad fontem ceruus, cum bibisset, restitit
et in liquore uidit effigiem suam.

Ibi dum ramosa mirans laudat cornua
crurumque nimiam tenuitatem uituperat,

uenantum subito uocibus conterritus
per campum fugere coepit et cursu leui
canes elusit.

Silua tum excepit ferum,
in qua retentis impeditus cornibus
lacerari coepit morsibus saeuis canum.

Tunc moriens edidisse uocem hanc dicitur,

"O me infelicem, qui nunc demum intellego
utilia mihi quam fuerint quae despexeram
et quae laudaram quantum luctus habuerint."

Phaedrus's cliché makes those gorgeous Antlers "branch" just in time to tangle in the trees. Don't you admire them?

39

HUNGER SHARPENS WITS WHEREVER THERE IS LIFE.

Anytime in the forest, suppose
supplies run short on the Bear.

He runs over to a rocky shore,
takes hold of a crag.
Softly gently lowers
shaggy legs into the pool.

In amongst the tufts there,
the moment crabs catch fast,
Bear whips them off to dry land.
Shakes out his prey from the sea.

Bear enjoys delicacies, gathered
from all over. Cunning itself.

Hunger sharpens wits,
you see. For fools, too.

: : :

FAMEM ACVERE ANIMANTIBVS INGENIVM

Si quando in siluis urso desunt copiae,

scopulosum ad litus currit et prendens petram
pilosa crura sensim demittit uado.

Quorum inter uillos simul haeserunt canceres,
in terram abripiens excutit praedam maris

escaque fruitur passim collecta uafer.

Ergo etiam stultis acuit ingenium fames.

Another "likely story" that doesn't make much of a story? This time we have no Greek version to blame for leaving us still hungry. Tale-less.

"Gotcha!" is also one way that fables *work.*

Modern folktale, and adverts, tell How Bears Fish, with their tails for rod.

40

No amount of good fortune can hide an ugly nature.

Jupiter, king of the gods, turned Vixen
into human form. There she sat,
a proper bride on her bed.

Saw a beetle creep from a corner.
Knew her old prey.
Pounced on it
in a trice.

Gods above! How they laughed: see her go!
The Almighty Father went red, gave up on Vixen.
Threw her out of the bedroom, seen off with this:

"There's a way of life that fits you: live it—
because you aren't fit to live up to my favors."

: : :

Naturam turpem nulla fortuna obtegit.

In humanam speciem cum uertisset Iuppiter uulpem,
legitimis ut sedit toris,

scarabaeum uidit prorepentem ex angulo,
notamque ad praedam celerius saliit.

Superi gradu risere. magnus erubuit pater,
uulpemque repudiatam thalamis expulit,

his prosecutus, "Viue quo digna es modo,
quia digna noſtris meritis non potes esse."

An unusually common Greek proverb kept insisting that "yellow doesn't suit a Ferret" (i.e., a weasel in a wedding dress).

This suggested the Greek version, starring the "Weasel Bride." All round Europe, weasel and ferret have been called "Lady" or "Bride" or "Momma," for good luck (*donna, numphitxa, comadrejà*).

Old Age and Death

41

Old Woman saw a Wine Jar lying drained.

Still best Falernian lees spread far and wide
a lovely aroma from its noble walls.

Voracious, she gulped this up, two nostrils' full.

Then said, "Blithe spirit, what good quality shall I
say that you had once, with remains like these?"

And, the relevance of this?
Whoever knows me will tell.

: : :

Anus iacere uidit epotam amphoram

adhuc Falerna faece ex testa nobili
odorem quae iucundum late spargeret.

Hunc poﬅquam totis auida traxit naribus,

"O suauis anima, quale te dicam bonum
antehac fuisse, tales cum sint reliquiae."

Hoc quo pertineat, dicet qui me nouerit.

Old Woman and Wine Jar: "Snap!" Yes, they made each other's meaning.

An "empty," or "broken," jar, according to a nasty enough run of Greek epigrams, sums up wine and women, when the party is over. And song.

A favorite Greek statue hunches Old Woman *significantly*, even *suggestively*, over a jar. Wasting marble on a waste of space that sums up the emptiness of pathos. Or, if you prefer, make that bathos.

Indescribable loss, anyhow, and Phaedrus not halfway through his *Fables*. This was the opener in his third book of five, just after he gave us something like an autobiography. Something riddling and teasing. You can see that he still wants to tell us about himself. You can tell he isn't going to.

"Blithe spirit" is a Latin pun, between aromatic "exhalation" and dear departed "soul" (*anima*). Old Women were the experts on booze and grief. It's not so clear that they smelled particularly keenly.

42

Up against all wild beasts,
and swift, Hound was brave.
Always did his master proud.

Sag set in, the crushing years.
One day, the moment came.

Sent out to fight bristling boar,
he grabbed an ear. But his teeth,
his rotten teeth. Jaws let quarry go.
Infuriated Hunter told him off.

The veteran Hound hit back:
"What was it let you down?
It was my body, not my mind.
You praise what I was
if you damn what I am."

There.
Philetus,
my reason for writing
you see. Just beautiful.

: : :

Aduersus omnes fortis ueloces feras
canis cum domino semper fecisset satis,

languere coepit annis ingrauantibus.

Aliquando obiectus hispidi pugnae suis
arripuit aurem, sed cariosis dentibus

praedam dimisit. hic tunc uenator dolens
canem obiurgabat.

Cui latrans contra senex,
"Non te destituit animus, sed uires meae.
Quod fuimus laudas, si iam damnas quod sumus."

Hoc cur, Philete, scripserim, puchre uides.

Fable **41** followed Phaedrus's longest piece, a mazy account of Fable, of Aesop, and, in particular, of himself. (Explored in my book; see Further Reading.) It must be saying he feels out of juice, whatever his age.

Now **42**, the last piece that we have in the wreckage left of the last book, bows out whimpering that the Old Critter can't help being finished. It *may* have been his envoi, though even the hint of an addressee, "Philetus," is courtesy of a scholar's emendation.

At any rate, these framing fables are sharp jabs at us not to forget. It's so important for any wannabe Aesop to brandish Old Age—for nostalgia, pity, one-upmanship, experience, and final humiliation (= **41**–**46**).

43

Bull in a tight entrance.

Struggled with his horns.

Trouble getting in the stall.
His manoeuvering.

Calf tried showing how.

"Shh!" said Bull, "I knew it
before you were even born."

Straighten out the expert:
think Bull said this to you.

: : :

Angusto in aditu taurus luctans cornibus

cum uix intrare posset ad praesepia,
monstrabat uitulus quo se pacto flecteret.

"Tace," inquit, "ante hoc noui quam tu natus es."

Qui doctiorem emendat sibi dici putet.

44

HOW TO TAME RAW ADOLESCENCE.

A Father with a Wild Son in his home.

Once he'd withdrawn away from Father's sight
he'd treat the slaves to maximum beatings.
He was riding a red-hot pubescence.

So Aesop rattled this tale off to Sir:

> "Someone yoked Aging Ox to a bullock.
>
> He rejected a yoke that meant ill-matched necks.
> On the grounds of declining strength, his age.
>
> 'No need to fear,' the Farmer reassured.
> 'I don't tell you to work, but to tame him.
> He injures too many, with hoof and horn.'

You, too. Don't hold him with you at all times?
don't squash his raw temperament with mercy?
Then, mind, protests from the household will swell."

The treatment
for beastliness
is to handle it.

: : :

QVOMODO DOMANDA SIT FEROX IVVENTVS

Paterfamilias saeuum habebat filium.

Hic e conspectu cum patris recesserat,
uerberibus seruos afficiebat plurimis
et exercebat feruidam adulescentiam.

Aesopus ergo narrat hoc breuiter seni,

"Quidam iuuenco uetulum adiungebat bouem.

Is cum refugiens impari collo iugum
aetatis excusaret uires languidas,

'Non eſt quod timeas,' inquit illi ruſticus,
'non ut labores dico, sed ut iſtum domes,
qui calce et cornu multos reddit debiles.'

Et tu nisi iſtum tecum assidue retines
feroxque ingenium comprimis clementia,
uide ne querela maior accrescat domus."

Atrocitati mansuetudo eſt remedium.

45

Horse met Ass.

One a tyrant with trappings.
The other worn out with toils.

Horse was crossing his path.
Ass gave way, too slow.

"Whoa," Horse said,
"I'm only just reined back
from stamping hooves on you."

Shh. Ass kept hush.
And groaned as well,
the gods be my witness.

Horse soon broke down racing.
Wound up sent to the farm.
Ass saw him loaded with dung.

Mocked Horse, and here is the gist:
"What on earth has become of you?
Once, proud with trappings.
Now, come to the hell you scorned."

All you lucky ones, who
despise your fellow man:
Always remember that margin of error.
You never do know what you'll become.

: : :

Insolens phaleris asino occurrit equus,

qui fatigatus malis transeunti tardius dedit ueniam.

"Vix," inquit, "me teneo, ut non te rumpam calcibus."

Reticuit ille, et gemitu testatur deos.

Equus currendo ruptus paruo in tempore
ad uillam est missus. hunc onustum stercore
ut uidit asinus, tali eum irrisit uerbo,

"Quid tibi, gloriose quondam phaleris?
modo ad contemptam redisti miseriam."

Felices qui ullum despiciunt,
dubii meminisse debent,
quia nesciunt quid futuri sint.

46

Whenever previous honor is lost,
there's fun for faint-hearts as well.
Then the fall's heavy.
Downfall.

Zapped by years, sapped of strength, Lion
was down. Drew out his last breath.

Boar came to him, thunder in the tusks.
Smash. Took revenge for an old wrong.

Bull, soon, hostility in his horns.
Gored his foe's body.

Ass saw it,
the beast is assaulted, no comeback.
Used hooves, to hammer out the brow.

As Lion expired: "It humiliated me,
my insults from the brave. But you . . .
To have to bear you, nature's shame,
is death twice over, sure, so it seems."

: : :

Quicumque amisit dignitatem pristinam,
ignauis etiam iocus est in casu graui.

Defectus annis et desertus uiribus
leo cum iaceret spiritum extremum trahens,

aper fulmineis uenit ad eum dentibus
et uindicauit ictu ueterem iniuriam.

Infestis taurus mox confodit cornibus
hostile corpus.

Asinus, ut uidit ferum
impune laedi, calcibus frontem extudit.

At ille expirans, "Fortis indigne tuli
mihi insultare: te, Naturae dedecus,
quod ferre certe cogor, bis uideor mori."

47

WATCH HOW YOU'RE DOING. NOT BACK THEN, BUT NOW.

Butterfly was fluttering by.
Wasp came along into view.

"Fate, such cruel fate. While those bodies were alive
from whose remnants life breathed in us, what was I?
Persuasive in peace and braveheart in war,
in all departments I headed my peers.
Now all I am is powder-light dust that floats.
What were you? You were no more than a pack mule.
Now you hurt whom you choose, shooting your sting."

Wasp's quip fitted its ways:
"Look. Who we are, not were."

: : :

NON PRAETERITAM SED PRAESENTEM ASPICIENDAM ESSE FORTUNAM

Papilio uespam praeteruolitans uiderat.

"O sortem iniquam. dum uiuebant corpora,
quorum ex reliquiis animam nos accepimus,

ego eloquens in pace, fortis proeliis,
arte omni princeps inter aequalis fui.

En cuncta: leuitas putris et uolito cinis.

Tu qui fuisti mulus clitellarius,
quemcumque uisum est laedis infixo aculeo."

At uespa dignam moribus uocem edidit,

"Non qui fuerimus, sed qui nunc simus uide."

Reincarnation—as classical folklore? It seems far-fetched.
Maybe this is "fakelore." It's always hard to tell, to be sure.
Maybe we should be stung into looking for what fables are,
not were.
That's what this book wanted to be about. Has been.

48

One born to bad luck
completes the sad laps of their life.
And more.
Hard misery from fate
runs them down after their death.
As well.

Galli, weird priests of goddess Cybele,
would go round about begging a living.
Took Ass, as usual toting the baggage.

Ass expired, from toil and from multiple drubbings.
They flayed him, made their drums from his hide.

When somebody asked, what had they done
with their pet, the answer was something like this:

"After death he thought he would find peace. But
look: he's dead, and they drub on him still."

: : :

Qui natus est infelix non uitam modo
tristem decurrit, uerum post obitum quoque
persequitur illum dura fati miseria.

Galli Cybebes circum in quaestum ducere
asinum solebant baiulantem sarcinas.

Is cum labore et plagis esset mortuus
detracta pelle sibi fecerunt tympana.

Rogati mox a quodam, delicio suo
quidnam fecissent, hoc locuti sunt modo,

"Putabat se post mortem securum fore
—ecce aliae plagae congeruntur mortuo."

The *Galli* fable is found in Greek *Aesops*, too. They underline that liberation turns a slave into a "freedman," a status that still owes the former owner yet more.

These carnival priests' rules broke all social rules: they were castrated, went out begging alms, wore strange gear, yelled weird hymns, bashed strange percussion (*tympana* and *cymbala*).

Exultant, they traded freedom, social and personal identity, and even selfhood, for the love of their dominatrix Mother Goddess.

Poor Ass.

49

HOW FAR DO WOMEN TAKE FICKLENESS AND LUST? WELL?

Some Woman lost the husband she had loved, down through the years. Lowered his body into the tomb.

Then no way could be found to tear her from him.
She would spend her whole life mourning in the grave.
Which won her fair name, for a maid's chastity.

Meantime some robbers of the god Jupiter's shrine
have paid for their sacrilege. Nailed to the cross.

To stop anyone removing their mortal remains,
soldiers are stationed over the corpses, as guards.
Near the vault where the Woman had shut herself in.

Time passed. One of the guards was thirsty. He sought
water, at dead of night, from the slip of a maid
who, it chanced, was attending mistress at the time.
She was on her way to bed. You see, she'd stayed up
way into the night, and dragged her vigil out late.
The door was opened a crack. The Soldier peered in.
Glimpsed an exceptional, beautiful, female.

His mind is undone. On the spot, the fire is lit.
Lust ablaze spreads over the shameless creature.

Clever wit finds a thousand and one excuses
for opportunities to see her more often.

Caught by all this constant continual contact
she slowly got more submissive to the stranger.
Before too long, a tighter bond chained up her heart.

While he spent nights there, that conscientious guard,
a body went missing from one of the crosses.
Panicky Soldier revealed what's what to the Woman.

That angel the Woman says: "No need for your fear."
Hands her husband's body to be fixed on the cross.
No, he wouldn't be done for dereliction of duty.

So it was, foulness stormed the citadel of fair fame.

: : :

QVANTA SIT INCONSTANTIA ET LIBIDO MVLIERVM

Per aliquot annos quaedam dilectum uirum
amisit et sarcophago corpus condidit.

A quo reuelli nullo cum posset modo
et in sepulcro lugens uitam degeret,
claram assecuta est famam castae uirginis.

Interea fanum qui compilarant Iouis
cruci suffixi luerunt poenas numini.

Horum reliquias ne quis posset tollere,
custodes dantur milites cadauerum
monumentum iuxta mulier quo se incluserat.

Aliquando sitiens unus de custodibus
aquam rogauit media nocte ancillulam
quae forte dominae tunc assistebat suae
dormitum eunti. namque lucubrauerat
et usque in serum uigilias perduxerat.
Paulum reclusis foribus miles prospicit
uidetque egregiam et facie pulchra feminam.

Corruptus animus ilico succenditur
et uritur impudentis sensim cupiditas.

Sollers acumen mille causas inuenit
per quas uidere possit illam saepius.

Cotidiana capta consuetudine

paulatim facta est aduenae submissior,
mox artior reuinxit animum copula.

Hic dum consumit noctes custos diligens
desideratum est corpus ex una cruce.
Turbatus miles factum exponit mulieri.

At sancta mulier, "Non est quod timeas," ait
uirique corpus tradit figendum cruci,
ne subeat ille poenas neglegentiae.

Sic turpitudo laudis obsedit locum.

This heroine is usually known as "The Widow of Ephesus," from her appearance in Petronius's great Roman novel of sex and drugs and hyperbole, *Satyrica* (§§110–13). Mikhail Bakhtin famously enthused that the tale sums up the Novel's power to rejuvenate culture, "Life over Death." But back in Petronius, a wife blushes to hear it, whereas her husband groans—the officer in charge should have replaced the corpse on the cross with the woman's. And Phaedrus's, or is it Perotti's, "moral" doesn't sound much like jubilation.

Back in *Aesop* (the *Life of Aesop*, again, §129: Aesop is framed by the Delphians, but defiant in jail: see my note on **18**), Ploughman seduces fresh Widow, graveside, by posing as equally fresh Widower. His Oxen are rustled while he is otherwise engaged, and now he does have something to mourn. Same; different. That's what telling a Fable is all about.

There will be sleeping enough in the Grave.

Further Reading

Here are the main leads, if you want to find out more about Phaedrus, or about Aesop's fables generally, in their classical phase. Watch out for this last fable. Put here, it doesn't mean what monk Adhémar's medieval moral says (see below). I may be monkeying with you.

50

Snail found a mirror.

Saw it shine a treat,
fell right in love.

In no time, it climbed
upon the disk, began
to lick it over.

It looked to have done
nothing for it. Except

sully the sheen
with spit and muck.

Ape found the mirror
fouled this way. Said,

"Those who allow suchlike
to walk all over them,
deserve such treatment."

For Women
who marry stupid men.
Utterly useless husbands.

: : :

Coclea repperit speculum

quod dum nimium fulgere uidisset,
adamauit,

et ﬅatim ascendens super
eius orbem, coepit delingere.

Nil uero ei uisa eﬅ contulisse,
nisi ut splendorem saliuis sordibus pollueret.

Simia inuenit id taliter inquinatum, et ait,

"Qui talibus se calcari permittunt,
talia suﬅinere merentur."

Mulieribus quae se ﬅultis et inutilissimis uiris coniungunt.

First, work on Phaedrus—my work. A dozen of his Roman anecdotes, focused on monarchs and power, are studied at length in my book: *Telling Tales on Caesar: Roman Stories from Phaedrus* (Oxford, 2001). In a technical article, I try to estimate "Phaedrus' *Fables:* the original corpus," *Mnemosyne* 52 (1999), pp. 308–29.

There is a full bibliographical guide to Phaedrus's past glories: R. W. Lamb, *Annales Phaedriani 1596–1996: A Bibliography of Phaedrus* (Lowestoft, 1998).

In 1970, the all-important manuscript of Phaedrus ("P" after the first editor P. Pithou) was at length rediscovered: now Pierpont Morgan Library "M. 906": C. E. Finch, "*The Morgan Manuscript of Phaedrus,*" *American Journal of Philology* 92 (1971), pp. 301–7, and O. Zwierlein, "*Der Codex Pithoeanus des Phaedrus in der Pierpont Morgan Library,*" *Rheinisches Museum* 113 (1970), pp. 91–93.

And Phaedrus gets good measure in our best survey of classical fable: N. Holzberg, *The Ancient Fable: An Introduction* (Bloomington, Ind., 2002).

For reference to Aesop's fables in Classical Antiquity, we all use the compilation of B. E. Perry, *Aesopica: A Series of Texts Relating to Aesop or Ascribed to Him or Closely Connected with the Literary Tradition That Bears His Name,* vol. 1 (Illinois, 1952; vol. 2 left no trace). This is handily catalogued in Perry's edition of *Babrius and Phaedrus* (Cambridge, Mass., and London, 1965, in the Loeb Classical Library), which presents Perry's translation of Phaedrus (facing the Latin text: complete, and plain).

The main *Aesop* collection in Greek is translated by O. and R. Temple, *Aesop: The Complete Fables* (London, 1998, in the Penguin Classics series: 358 stories, including a bare half dozen of ours, in their Greek [non-Phaedrian] variants).

The tangle of medieval prose paraphrases of Phaedrus was captured in five wonderful doorstop volumes by R. Hervieux, *Les fabulistes latins depuis le siècle d'Auguste jusqu'à la fin du Moyen Age* (Paris, 1883–89, 1894[2]; reprinted, Hildesheim, 1970). One was likely by the monk, educationalist, and future historian Adhémar, "one of the success stories of the eleventh century" (R. Landes, *Relics, Apocalypse and the Deceits of History: Ademar of Chábannes, 981–1034* (Cambridge, Mass., 1995) at p. 52; cf. F. Bertini, *Il monaco Ademaro e la sua Raccolta di Favole fedriane* [Genoa, 1975]).

The so-called *Appendix Perottina* supplies fifteen of the stories in this book. Archbishop Niccolò Perotti's monster ragbag of fables and the like, serving up harmless beginners' Latin for all the children, includes thirty-two otherwise long lost poems of Phaedrus, jumbled and streamlined (including fable **2**, and an odd fragment of editorial). He was a fascinating Renaissance Man, but there is nothing to read on him in English: M. Furno, *Le "cornu copiae," de Niccolò Perotti: Culture et méthode d'un humaniste qui aimait les mots* (Geneva, 1995); S. Boldrini, *Fedro e Perotti: Richerche di storia della tradizione* (Urbino, 1990).

Add in La Fontaine, L'Estrange, Lessing . . . through Disney, and it starts to dawn how these stories string together the civilization of the West. The hands they have passed through!

The Butchers Coat of Arms

Indexes

It is not so ugly as a purse-proud, ignorant, wicked man.

Tables for the Fables

Aesop's Human Zoo and Phaedrus, and Aesopica

KEY

Bold numbers **1** through **50** as in *Aesop's Human Zoo.*

Numbers 1.1 through 5.10 as in most editions of Phaedrus's *Fables.*

A.1 through A.32 = *Perotti's Appendix,* a bunch of Phaedrian fables known only through a Renaissance collector's trimmed versions (see above, *Further Reading*).

AES = *Aesopic Fables* numbered as in Perry's compilation (see Further Reading). Numbers below 472 extant in Greek versions; numbers over 472 not extant in Greek, but in Phaedrus and, over 557, in PhP.

PhP = Phaedrian fables known only through a set of medieval prose paraphrases. My texts follow the half-preserved original verses where possible, and otherwise present a composite of medieval and "corrected" Latin (see Further Reading).

1 = Phaedrus 1.Prologue
2 = A.3 [The stuff of Greek sermons]
3 = A.5 [AES. 535: but from Greek proverb]
4 = 1.18 [AES. 479: but in Greek in Plutarch's *Marriage Guidance*]
5 = 1.19 [AES. 480: but probably from Greek]
6 = A.19 [AES. 547]
7 = 3.15 [AES. 506]
8 = 4.15 [AES. 515a]
9 = 4.16 [AES. 515b: but in Greek in Lucian's *You Verbal Prometheus*]
10 = 3.3 [AES. 495: but in Greek in Plutarch's *Seven Sages' Party*]
11 = 4.17 [AES. 516]
12 = A.11 [AES. 539: but from Greek]
13 = 1.24 [AES. 376; cf. 371]
14 = A.13 [AES. 541]
15 = PhP [AES. 564]
16 = 1.26 [AES. 426: in Greek from Plutarch's *Party Quiz*]
17 = A.25 [AES. 552: but in Greek, e.g., with chameleon and snake, in Aelian's *Zoology*]
18 = PhP [AES. 384]
19 = A.32 [AES. 557]
20 = PhP [AES. 566: but cf. 172 and Greek proverb]
21 = 1.7 [AES. 27; Greek proverb]
22 = 3.4 [AES. 496]
23 = 3.8 [AES. 499: but in Greek, e.g., in Plutarch's *Party Quiz*]
24 = A.17 [AES. 545]
25 = 1.11 [AES. 151]
26 = PhP [AES. 572]
27 = 3.18 [AES. 509]
28 = 2.2 [AES. 31]
29 = 5.6 [AES. 528: but from Greek proverbs]
30 = A.4 [AES. 534]
31 = 3.11 [AES. 502]
32 = A.30 [AES. 118]
33 = A.1 [AES. 533]
34 = 4.19 [AES. 517: but probably from Greek]
35 = 1.29 [AES. 484]
36 = PhP [cf. AES. 130]
37 = PhP [AES. 302]
38 = 1.12 [AES. 74]
39 = A.22 [AES. 550]
40 = PhP [but cf. AES. 50/107]
41 = 3.1 [AES. 493]
42 = 5.10 [AES. 532]
43 = 5.9 [AES. 531]
44 = A.12 [AES. 540]
45 = PhP [AES. 565: but cf. AES. 318; from Greek proverb]
46 = 1.21 [AES. 481: but probably from Greek]
47 = A.31 [AES. 556]
48 = 4.1 [AES. 164]
49 = A.15 [AES. 543: but cf. AES. 388]
50 = PhP [AES. 559]

PHAEDRUS 1.PROLOGUE = **1**

1.7 = **21**
1.11 = **25**
1.12 = **38**
1.18 = **4**
1.19 = **5**
1.21 = **46**
1.24 = **13**
1.26 = **16**
1.29 = **35**
2.2 = **28**
3.1 = **41**
3.3 = **10**
3.4 = **22**
3.8 = **23**
3.11 = **31**
3.15 = **7**
3.18 = **27**
4.1 = **48**
4.15 = **8**
4.16 = **9**
4.17 = **11**
4.19 = **34**
5.6 = **29**
5.9 = **43**
5.10 = **42**
A.1 = **33**
A.3 = **2**
A.4 = **30**
A.5 = **3**
A.11 = **12**
A.12 = **44**
A.13 = **14**
A.15 = **49**
A.17 = **24**
A.19 = **6**
A.22 = **39**
A.25 = **17**
A.30 = **32**
A.31 = **47**
A.32 = **19**
PhP = **15**, **18**, **20**, **26**, **36**, **37**, **40**, **45**, **50**.
AES. 27 = **21**
AES. 31 = **28**
AES. 50 = **40**
AES. 74 = **38**
AES. 107 = **40**
AES. 118 = **32**
AES. 130 = **36**
AES. 151 = **25**
AES. 164 = **48**
AES. 302 = **37**
AES. 376 = **13**
AES. 384 = **18**
AES. 388 = **49**
AES. 426 = **16**
AES. 479 = **4**
AES. 480 = **5**
AES. 481 = **46**
AES. 484 = **35**
AES. 493 = **41**
AES. 495 = **10**
AES. 496 = **22**
AES. 499 = **23**
AES. 502 = **31**
AES. 506 = **7**
AES. 509 = **27**
AES. 515a = **8**
AES. 515b = **9**
AES. 517 = **34**
AES. 528 = **29**
AES. 531 = **43**
AES. 532 = **42**
AES. 533 = **33**
AES. 534 = **30**
AES. 535 = **3**
AES. 539 = **12**
AES. 540 = **44**
AES. 541 = **14**
AES. 543 = **49**
AES. 545 = **24**
AES. 547 = **6**
AES. 550 = **39**
AES. 552 = **17**
AES. 556 = **47**
AES. 557 = **19**
AES. 559 = **50**
AES. 564 = **15**
AES. 565 = **45**
AES. 566 = **20**
AES. 572 = **26**

The Cast of Characters

(Numbers are fable numbers rather than page numbers)

Tempting Topics

(Numbers are fable numbers)